VILLAGES IN THE SUN

MEDITERRANEAN COMMUNITY ARCHITECTURE

VILLAGES IN THE SUN

MEDITERRANEAN COMMUNITY ARCHITECTURE

MYRON GOLDFINGER
FOREWORD BY LOUIS I. KAHN
PHOTOGRAPHS BY THE AUTHOR

RIZZOLI
NEW YORK

Revised and redesigned color edition first published
in the United States of America in 1993 by
Rizzoli International Publications, Inc.
300 Park Avenue South, New York, New York 10010

Library of Congress Cataloging-in-Publication Data

Goldfinger, Myron.
Villages in the sun : Mediterranean community architecture /
by Myron Goldfinger ; with a preface by Louis I. Kahn.
p. cm.
Originally published : New York : Praeger, 1969.
ISBN 0-8478-1528-5. — ISBN 0-8478-1529-3 (pbk.)
1. City planning—Mediterranean Region. 2. Architects and
community—Mediterranean Region. I. Title.
NA9184.M4G6 1993
711'.4'091822—dc20   92-40715
                                      CIP

Designed by Pamela Fogg
Printed and bound in Singapore

Front cover: Santorini, Greece
Frontispiece: Paraportiani Church, Mykonos, Greece
Back cover: Djerba, Tunisia

CONTENTS

MAP 6

ACKNOWLEDGMENTS 7

A COMMUNITY ARCHITECTURE 8

FOREWORD BY LOUIS KAHN 9

PREFACE 10

INTRODUCTION 12

GREECE 26
MYKONOS 28
SERIFOS 36
SANTORINI 38
SKYROS 46
SIFNOS 56
POST-BYZANTINE CHURCHES OF THE AEGEAN ISLANDS 60
PARAPORTIANI CHURCH ON MYKONOS 68

ITALY 72
PROCIDA 74
ALBEROBELLO 84
POSITANO 90

CORSICA 92

SPAIN 94
MIJAS 96
BENALMÉDENA 104
ARCOS DE LA FRONTERA 106
VEJER DE LA FRONTERA 112
GUADIX 114
CUEVAS DEL ALMANZORA 120

MOROCCO 122
VILLAGE NEAR TIZI-N-TICHKA PASS 124
VILLAGE IN THE OURIKA VALLEY 128
AIT-BENHADDOU 130
KSOURS IN THE DADES VALLEY 138
OASIS OF TINERHIR 140
VILLAGE NEAR KHENIFRA 148

TUNISIA 150
MATMATA 152
GHORFAS AT METAMEUR AND GHOUMRASSEN HADADA 158
TAKROUNA 166
MOSQUES OF DJERBA 172

1	Mykonos	14	Guadix
2	Serifos	15	Cuevas del Almanzora
3	Santorini	16	Village near Tizi-n-Tichka Pass
4	Skyros	17	Village in the Ourika Valley
5	Sifnos	18	Ait-Benhaddou
6	Procida	19	Tinerhir
7	Alberobello	20	Village near Khenifra
8	Positano	21	Matmata
9	Bonifacio, Corsica	22	Metameur
10	Mijas	23	Ghoumrassen Hadada
11	Benalmédena	24	Takrouna
12	Arcos de la Frontera	25	Djerba
13	Vejer de la Frontera		

ACKNOWLEDGMENTS

Life is a great adventure, and for those fortunate to live in this age, the opportunity to travel so easily to distant places is unique. And so June and I travelled and experienced the Mediterranean on our three-month honeymoon, and we saw the great architecture presented in this book.

Thank you, June, for putting up with what is not evident in the photographs: the 120-degree heat of the Tunisian desert, the dangerous roadways of the Ronda Mountains, the arrival at Sifnos at two in the morning from a listing ship, the desert coyotes howling in a remote village in Morocco, the detention for five hours by Algerian border guards, the broken auto fan while we were deep in the valley of the Draa, and much, much more.

I did not have the opportunity to travel in my youth. But I have had the great pleasure of seeing my daughters travel and explore distant places at a young age—Thira in China and Djerba in Russia—places further than I have reached. I wish those who study this book the joy of travel and discovery of their own.

I also wish to acknowledge my mother and father, Bertha and William Goldfinger, two beautiful and humble people, who by their early devotion, have inspired and will continue to inspire me throughout my life; to Louis Kahn, the greatest architect of this half-century, whose teachings and works enlightened me; to Sibyl Moholy-Nagy and Bernard Rudofsky, who through their works and personal contact have guided my work for this book; to the Ford Foundation and the Architectural League of New York for their assistance in the completion of my research; and to David Morton and the Rizzoli staff for having a special interest in this work and the desire to republish it in new form and color.

And finally, thanks to the great anonymous builders of the Mediterranean, who made it so easy to photograph, so reasonable to believe, yet so mystical to interpret.

I dedicate this voyage
to the Mediterranean
to my wife June
and to my daughters
Thira and Djerba.

A COMMUNITY ARCHITECTURE

A community architecture must provide for
the means of communication
which can enrich and substantiate
a true building art.
Communal architectural survival
must go hand in hand with a spirit of
touch, see, and be.
Barriers can only divide
and cause aloneness and aloofness.
A community architecture starts in the streets,
extends into the parks,
and reaches the rivers.
It depends on public response for its very existence
and therefore reflects the will of the people.
What is achieved is a place for human experience,
a rich variety of forms and spaces
in which to live,
a structural framework which permits
the expression of the individual,
and the participation of all.

Myron Goldfinger, 1969

FOREWORD

Prevailance of order
Prevailance of commonness
Being is of order
Desire to be of order is life
To live is to express.

The spare atmosphere of Mars tells us of this prevailance to be;
not of the attitude not of the choice, the vectors to the character
of living forms and shapes.
In outer space the Earth is felt in wonder as if for the first time.
This marble, blue-green and rose, unique in our system makes us
realize that man's work can be like no other.

The builder seeking a beginning is primed by
his feelings of commonness and the inspirations of Nature.

Just a fragment of knowing steers wonder to intuition and
to the acts of expression. In the presence of the mountain
the water the wind the desire to express feels the possible.
The site confirms the possible and encourages agreement
on the beginning in the making of a man's place.
A mere foothold is confident of the settlement,
the first institution of man.

The works of man reveal his nature.

The time of a work holds its own validity from
which the sense of truth can be drawn to inspire
a work of another time.

The city from a simple settlement became the place
of the assembled institutions.

The measure of the greatness of a city must come from
the character of its institutions established by those
sensitive to commonness and dedication to man's desire for
higher levels of expression.

The places of the island the hamlet the mountain
draws us to them for their simple truth.

To leave them for the city must bring
revived faith in new beginning.
A city must ever be greater and greater.

Commonness is the spirit Art
A work of art is an offering to Art.

Louis Kahn, 1969

PREFACE

It is now almost twenty-five years since the original black-and-white edition of *Villages in the Sun* was first published. Much has transpired in this quarter century. Conservation and preservation efforts have saved some natural lands from development and certain historic edifices from destruction. The historicists of the 1980s, who peppered both urban and rural areas with theatrical imitations of the past, have finally reached their limits. And Louis Kahn, one of the greatest and most admired architects of this century, is gone, leaving a legacy of work, dreams, and ideas.

Architects are molded by both the refined and the organic buildings of the past, but it is the unique assemblage of structures dedicated to contemporary needs that defines the elements and forms of new developments and the restoration of older neighborhoods. Architecture has always been more than the clever manipulation of the past, but simple, traditional truths are still its guides. In addition, natural construction processes—the organization of plant life, the building systems of the animal kingdom—should serve as resources, as should the strength and integrity of efficient and powerful early building.

I have interpreted the spirit of the architecture of the Mediterranean, discovered through travel and research, in my own work, shown here. Vernacular buildings have helped me to understand honesty in structure, basic geometry in form, repetitive elements in massing, and most importantly, the noble quality of defined space for living, work, and recreation.

I hope that this new color, revised edition of *Villages in the Sun* will inspire more honest and spiritual future architectural works. And I look forward to a more sensitive understanding and appreciation of structural form, of building in the landscape, and of urban harmony, as reflected in the indigenous architecture of the Mediterranean.

New York, 1992

Covecastles, Anguilla, West Indies

House, Waccabuc, New York

House, Montague, New Jersey

House, Sands Point, New York

House, Long Island, New York

INTRODUCTION

In architecture today, many branches of design have become separated from their roots; additionally, poor building results from a lack of understanding of fundamental problems and from a superficial adaptation of expedient solutions. While our knowledge of technology and psychology has increased, we have generally not applied these new techniques and methods to building, nor have we substantially increased our understanding of the basic problems of shelter.

Builders, politicians, and business-oriented architects are not alone at fault. A generation of serious architects has misunderstood and misinterpreted the social and psychological needs of the people. They have failed to make a significant contribution to housing, and they have not effectively guided public opinion, which is essential to the promotion of new ideas. Only now is a new generation of architects beginning to respond to this urgent need in a meaningful way, with thought, research, and determination.

Before this century of greatly accelerated achievement, people had built their habitats of local materials, strongly, naturally, simply. Their plans were direct and certain, based on function and necessity. And they took pride in their structures.

Now, with the confusion of mass materials and mass building, and in response to technological development, population growth, and urban centralization, this direct relationship has been terminated. But despite demands for rapid solutions to the need for more housing, it is important not to forget our relationship to the sun, the wind, the rain, and the land, the social and psychological demands of our society, and the ingenious ways people have for centuries sheltered themselves. Through research into the valid aspects of an earlier community architecture, we can discover the basic roots of its development and proceed with an enlarged vocabulary and clearer ideas for better planning and building of our own urban communities.

Today, two major problems are raised by the changing conditions within our cities. First, there is a lack of cohesive order and sound judgment in the multiplicity of isolated structures; speculative ventures have created a disorder of anonymous high-rise residential structures in the midst of our urban centers. Second, the vast development of these anonymous public residential structures has created large and monotonous expanses of building conformity which lacks the vital ingredients for the enhancement of living. Together, these extreme conditions have completely destroyed neighborhood patterns and identity and have drastically affected the society of the original residents while achieving nothing for the new urbanites. There is absolutely no feeling for urban unity and even less feeling for the urban community.

And another blight has developed around our cities. The once harmonious landscape has been transformed and distorted by endless and anonymous suburban villages. The search for escape from polluted and claustrophobic urban living conditions has led many city dwellers to seek refuge in peripheral areas. In addition, the vastly accelerated urban-center population growth, coupled with the lack of adequate rebuilding programs within our cities, has created a demand for even more perimeter housing. Speculative builders have catered to the immediate needs and financial capabilities of the desperate populace and have bulldozed vast acreage adjacent to our cities into grids of separate but identical units stretching endlessly across former farmland and forest, hill and marsh, creating continuous monostructures of isolated cells. Separation and isolation, uniformity and conformity, oneness and sameness are the banal standards for luxury and middle- and low-income suburban planning and building, as they are in almost all urban areas.

In our search to improve our conditions, we should look for spiritual guidance to the towns and villages of the Mediterranean: contained communities similar in size and scale to our urban neighborhoods and new suburban villages. Mediterranean villages have developed organically within economical and repetitive forms whose roots are similar to our own community structures. What is achieved is a harmonious working arrangement with the site: accommodating rather than pompously destroying it, building rather than levelling it, defining rather than distorting it. What is achieved is a place for human experience, a rich variety of forms and spaces in which to live, and a structural framework that permits expression of the individual and participation of the whole community.

This book is intended to serve as an introduction to the vernacular architecture of the Mediterranean. I have chosen what I consider to be the most representative examples of the numerous villages that reflect the culture of the popular Mediterranean builders. Many factors relate these villages conceptually, partly due to the centuries of trade and conquest that have diffused ideas and forms. However, the overall common bond has been the honest, intelligent, and natural way the problem of shelter has been solved.

We cannot repeat the Mediterranean structures; we do not want to repeat particular designs. New social demands require new approaches; new materials require new responses; new technology requires new creativity. However, human needs persist: the needs for shelter, for storage, for privacy, and for communal experience; the needs for air, for sun and warmth, for nature to enjoy and respect. These obvious, simple requirements will remain no matter how technological and sophisticated our societies may become. It is my hope that our architecture and our planning will respect these demands, that a humanism in architecture will create not an artificial picturesqueness or quaintness but sound and strong statements reaffirming the dignity of people and demonstrating their progress.

HISTORY

Since ancient times, communities have been formed for protection, economy, and human companionship. The earliest villagers built with local materials on protective sites or burrowed within the earth itself. A constant and organic development of shelter has occurred in all parts of the world. Although certain characteristics have evolved in response to such natural conditions as climatic changes, earth composition, and water resources, artificial political or racial boundaries have never distinguished building types. In forested areas, people lived in trees or built from wood; in rocky regions, in caves or from stone. While there was occasionally an abundance of natural wealth, limited resources often encouraged people to discover and work with simple, available materials. Therefore, it is not surprising that humans in many regions of the world, although isolated by bodies of water or mountain ranges, would arrive at similar solutions to identical problems.

ISOLATED UNITS

The nucleus for the development of the village form has been the isolated unit or house, which eventually became the basic unit of habitation or housing type. This unit was developed primarily in response to the need for protection from extremes of temperature, from rain or snow storms and strong winds, and from enemies, both human and animal. In addition, the isolated unit provided storage for food and tools, as well as shelter for domestic animals. In the earliest dwellings, these demands were met in a single, simple space with a solitary access door and perhaps an additional ventilation opening. As life became more complex, additional rooms were constructed, sometimes vertically, by adding levels, sometimes horizontally, by building more units or dividing the basic volume. Forms always evolved from interior spatial requirements, and the size, shape, and means of access of the dwellings also re-

flected specific functions. External influences affected the plan as well. The atrium or courtyard house was developed in response to the need for a private, protected outdoor workroom or family space; a steep hillside suggested a multilevel plan to take advantage of the contours; flooding conditions at rivers or seashores determined a dwelling type raised on pilings.

VILLAGE DEVELOPMENT

Family or tribal groups often banded together for collective work or defense, and communities were formed of individual units either separated or, more often, attached in rows or clusters. This new relationship limited unit expansion, but the advantages of community, both social and related to building, outweighed the disadvantages of isolation. Materials were gathered collectively; scaffolding was reused; more tools were available; common paths were constructed. The atrium house gained a new function: it provided privacy more than protection. Other dwelling types, with projecting balconies and roof terraces, were developed to compensate for territorial limitations. In each instance, though, a sound economic and social basis for the development of a community superseded such considerations as privacy, unit expansion, and individual expression. Therefore, within the established structural framework, zoning for privacy was introduced, maximum utilization of space was intensified, and a search for individual identity was established. This encouraged new approaches toward both the living experience and the building process, and promoted the development of new solutions in response to new challenges.

VILLAGE CHARACTERISTICS

From their earliest development, communities formulated very different characteristics in relation to such local and regional traits as topography, climate, and available materials, and to the social requirements of personal livelihood, family groups, and community organization. Although there is great variety in social form and town organization, certain basic attributes common to all vernacular villages may be identified. There are six major areas through which any of the communities may be analyzed: their relationship to their natural environment, an organized town composition, negative spaces, habitation units, exceptional buildings, and appropriate materials and detailing.

Relationship to the natural environment. The first important consideration is the unique relationship of a village to its natural surroundings; it is necessary to balance the two. A dominant landscape demands a deferential village form; flat, spacious surroundings welcome a powerful, sculptural configuration. Generally, there are two types of villages: the organic and the articulated. Organic villages relate more closely to their natural environment. The most obvious are cave communities, which are virtually one with the earth. In some instances, openings and light and ventilation shafts, highlighted by their form and color, pierce the surface, but these openings enrich rather than disturb the natural form, and an overall harmony with nature is preserved. Villages built of local materials left in their natural state also relate very closely to their surroundings. Some, built on precipices or hills, actually accentuate the terrain and thereby reinforce the natural form.

The second type, the articulated village, is expressed separately from its natural environment either by its form or its use of color. For instance, although the tone and texture of the village's buildings may be the same as its earth base, their scale and configuration create a dynamic massing that often dominates the natural topography. Individual units might be painted white or a reflective color that clearly distinguishes the community from its surroundings. However, village forms generally follow the contours of the terrain—be it hill, peninsula, or water's edge—and thus still create a distinct yet harmonious relationship with their sites.

Organized town composition. The second common feature is an overall unity and density of village form. Urbanism is achieved by close association of like building forms, economically conceived within site limitations. Although a village may take a linear, terraced configuration on a hill or a clustered configuration in a valley, its individual components form a tight, unified plan. Villages generally develop in relation to a single large negative space that may serve spiritual or commercial needs—a harbor, river, oasis, or town square—and that may provide the setting for one or more exceptional buildings, with strong forms that are highlighted by the backdrop of similar dwellings.

Negative spaces. Paths, streets, bridges, and tunnels defined by habitations link the units and also direct traffic to the harbor, town square, or local public center. These passages form a progression of spaces that express function and movement. Their length and width depend on circulation needs as well as on natural limitations. Negative spaces, varying in size and shape, also naturally organize community life. A dynamic vitality is created by the interaction of different people in different spaces. Wider passages become market streets, since a constant flow toward a nucleus encourages the natural development of commerce. Lower floors of houses are often converted into shops; thus the commercial establishment fuses with the living quarters to create a family enterprise, similar to those still existing in some form in our modern cities and towns.

In addition, neighborhood squares appear along the streets, like small courtyards defined by dwellings and serving these perimeter inhabitants. Larger plazas serve larger groupings. A combination of courtyards and plazas relieves the repetition of the unit form and creates alcoves along the passages that provide order, direction, and an important sense of place.

Each type of open space serves a different need: The narrowest paths offer protection from strong winds and harsh sun, and provide a psychologically soothing intimacy where neighbors can be close to one another. The local plaza or courtyard serves as a playground for the young and a meeting place for all within a protected, shaded environment. The major square is where the action is; it serves as combination business center, festive hall, promenade, visual focus, and link with the outside world.

Habitation units. The most important element in any village is the basic living unit, which functions in two important ways. First, it is a family shelter, providing reasonable individual expression and the amenities unique to the region. Second, it is the primary element in a cellular system of orderly growth that permits free expansion and contraction of the village form without disturbing the unity of the whole.

The housing unit, when repeated in relation to natural conditions, also delineates outdoor spaces and defines the physical expression of the village. Generally, the buildings are attached or semi-detached; their plans vary according to specific needs within the limitations of the unit. Constant features are a major living space, sleeping areas, and a kitchen-and-work space. In addition, each dwelling has some kind of outdoor space: interior courtyard, front or rear yard, or roof terrace. Occasionally, a protruding balcony or recessed porch is built to meet a specific requirement.

A great efficiency of design characterizes the dwellings. All spaces, interior and exterior, are simply and economically conceived; none is wasted or misused. Available materials determine the structure; a lack of wood or metal, for instance, produces variations in vaulted roof forms, which may be barrel vaults, cones, or cupolas. In some villages, these roof shapes become the dominant visual element of the community. In others, roofs are covered and flattened to achieve a more useful surface for work, recreation, and the drying of food, household materials, and clothing. In these villages, articulation of the wall surfaces receives more emphasis, creating a cubic geometry.

Exceptional buildings. In some villages, dynamic siting, a contained harbor, or a large inner square relieves the repetition of the unit architectural form. But within the overall plan, singular buildings serve either as pivot points in the streetscape or as terminal foci for the town. Since political and social life in Mediterranean villages tends to center around religion, these buildings are usually churches or chapels. In communities where a more personal religion predominates, abundant chapels appear among the dwellings. The simplest of these structures share the architecture of houses but are distinguished by contrasting roofs that may include bell towers or minarets. Other chapels are individual, sculptural forms that express on the exterior their particular internal functions and are visual attractions throughout the village.

Larger chapels or village churches occupy prominent positions and dominate the major squares. In some communities they are located at the highest point and are identifiable from great distances. The strong plastic form of these structures presents a necessary contrast to the relative uniformity of the repeated dwelling unit, because even well-planned communities of like structures create a monotony that can be relieved only by the exceptional building.

Materials and detailing. The sixth major consideration of all vernacular villages is the honest derivation of the forms, textures, and colors of the surfaces and details of the buildings. Sizes, shapes, and locations of openings in the walls and roofs demonstrate the need for light, ventilation, and the movement of people, animals, and goods. Therefore, living areas have larger windows, while sleeping chambers have only small openings, primarily for ventilation. The door is sized according to its function. A wide opening or double door is provided for animals or large carts; otherwise, the door is designed to accommodate only people. When it is open, the door also admits additional light and ventilation to the interior. Finally, all openings are normally positioned in relation to sun orientation and wind direction.

Roof surfaces have always provided psychological security as well as actual protection. In many villages, roof forms and textures are quite pronounced and are an important means of expression. The use of stone, thatch, or paint over cement has made the roof surface an important natural decorative element in unit design.

Wall textures and colors relate directly to climatic conditions. Stucco is applied for protection from moisture; whitewash is employed primarily for its heat-reflective qualities. Paint is used to protect exterior wood surfaces, such as doors, window frames, stairs, and balconies; this is one reason why the builders choose these particular areas for their own individual expressions of color and decorative design. Interiors are generally painted white or a light color to reflect the limited interior light. Built-in wood furniture or extensions of stone exterior walls are common within dwelling units and serve to unify the interior spaces. Utilitarian objects and planters are hung on the walls, set on the floors, and placed in recessed niches to provide an impressive sculptural display against the neutral surfaces, both inside and out. In addition, personal possessions—framed photographs, drawings, paintings, and decorative plates—decorate the interior walls. Any variations in detailing strongly express individual identity; they do not destroy the basic unity but rather add an overall richness and vitality.

INDIVIDUAL NEEDS/COMMUNITY NEEDS

Important psychological considerations are reflected in the design of vernacular houses and villages. Within the dwelling is a need for privacy; in addition, each room requires certain spatial relationships. Amenities such as courtyards, terraces, roof gardens, and balconies, which may have been conceived as work spaces rather than as social centers, play an important role in creating a dynamic and variable diversity of spaces. Because of their involvement in their houses—as designers, builders, crafters—the inhabitants have a great deal invested in their dwellings and express it freely within the framework of individual units. Villagers also work together on public projects. The synthesis of building for individuals, families, and communities has led to the creation of appropriately scaled villages with a diversity and interesting spatial relationships that grow from honest, creative uses of materials, methods, and site. This fact underlies the building process of vernacular villages throughout the Mediterranean area.

DWELLING TYPES

Vernacular villages are generally composed of either negative or positive houses. Negative habitations are found in, hollowed in, or excavated from the earth. Certain geological and climatic conditions promote shelters with little or no actual construction; these dwellings are truly a part of the natural terrain and disturb the landscape only very subtly. Positive habitations, on the other hand, are buildings constructed above the surface of the earth from locally available materials. Although both types work in harmony with the landscape, positive structures stand erect and distinguish themselves as totally artificial rather than as developments of a subterranean formation. Many combinations of the two types exist in order to take full advantage of the local geography.

CAVE DWELLINGS

Among the early types of housing, the simplest and most economical are cave or earth dwellings, which provide protection from animals, enemies, rain, snow, wind, and extremes of heat and cold. Early underground habitations have been discovered in such areas as China, Turkey, Italy, Tunisia, and the United States. Many are still occupied today. Just as there are many types of surface buildings, there are variations in subterranean habitations, from the simplest natural cave to the completely artificial underground complex. Invariably, differences occur because of the natural earth composition. When the rock is hard and difficult to work, the cave remains unaltered; with soft rock or better tools, natural forms are changed.

Four types of underground dwellings are common: natural caves, altered natural caves, altered natural caves with additions, and artificial caves. The primary type is the natural cave, where early people settled. The exterior is inconspicuous; the interior varies with natural conditions. Some caves are quite small, with just enough space for one person or a small family, while others contain extensive caverns with multiple entrances and were once inhabited by whole tribes.

In areas with easily workable rock, individual natural caves were sometimes connected to form a network of tunnels and chambers, such as seen in the steep cliffs at Pantalica, Sicily. In addition, voids in rock that had been eroded by winds and rain were enlarged and developed. At Göreme, in the Anatolian region of Turkey, conical mounds of volcanic rock have been transformed into complex apartment dwellings that are still inhabited.

At Guadix, Spain, inhabitants hollowed out additions to their cave dwellings from the soft rock and also added structures to the faces of the caves. Clusters of white, conical chimneys were built to ventilate the interiors; white stucco walls were built to define private yards and to retain earth. In the southwestern United States and in the Lascaux region of France, too, early cliff dwellers added to the surface of their cave dwellings.

The most unusual type of cave house is the entirely artificial cavity excavated from the earth, with private chambers dug around the perimeter. At Matmata, Tunisia, the caves are large oval cavities, sometimes two hundred feet in diameter and thirty feet deep, in which up to one hundred people live. Long ramp-tunnels extend from ground level to the bottom of the cavities. A similarly scaled underground village with a quite different configuration exists near Tongguan, in the Honan Province of China. It is composed of well-defined squares carved out of loess arranged in crisp, geometric patterns with L-shaped staircases that lead to the dwellings. In both cases, the flat plains above the villages serve as their farmland.

FABRICATED BUILDING TYPES

Almost every available natural material has been used in the construction of shelters: snow and ice are the building blocks of the Eskimo igloo; animal skins supported by wood posts are employed for the portable tent of the desert nomad. Climatic extremes and isolation have produced ingenious solutions and thus a great variety of building types. However, most positive structures developed by the vernacular builder can be classified into four general types: reed, wood, wood-masonry, and masonry.

Reed structures. The lightest, easiest to build, and least permanent buildings are the reed structures that are indigenous to tropical regions and also found in many temperate areas. These structures are disposable or portable and are the oldest style of constructed building. Reed fibers are both flexible and strong and can be twisted, tied together, and bent into domed, conical, or barrel-vaulted units of considerable strength and rigidity. Layers of thatch, leaves, or skins usually serve as protective roofing. The size of the unit is determined by the diameter of the hoop frame, which varies in response to individual needs and to the fiber strength. This construction method leads to a plan of independent units with a single main space and only limited provision for expansion. Villages are established by grouping these units into a protective ringed enclosure around an oval central outdoor space. This is one of the earliest village forms and has been the model for the development of most defensive towns and villages throughout history.

Wood structures. Wood is considerably stronger and more durable than reed. One of its earliest uses was by Swiss lake dwellers who built defensive villages on pilings in the lakes; they were connected to the mainland by bridges. Although vulnerable to fire, strong windstorms, and termites, timber structures can be constructed rapidly and today account for most of the small houses in the United States, Scandinavia, and Japan. Most villages constructed from timber are formed of individual units, since common buttressing walls are not needed; in addition, separate houses are more easily protected from fire. The arrangement of communities composed by wood buildings consists, for the most part, of isolated but related units. Some advantages of wood construction are an ease of alteration in response to changing needs and relatively quick repair in the event of damage or destruction. The rich forests of New England prompted the development of colonial America's boxy, wood houses. Examples of this building type are the fishing shacks along the seacoasts of Massachusetts and Maine, as well as farm structures inland. Wood structures at Palheiros de Tocha on the Portuguese coast, on pilings on the beach for protection from high tides, are similar but built into a more cohesive village form.

Wood-masonry structures. The wood-masonry structure is common in regions where both materials are generally available. Masonry is used for foundations and supporting walls because of its strength and durability, either in the form of stone or rock cut or broken into easily workable sizes and shapes, or of sun-dried clay bricks. The joints are sometimes mortared but often the masonry is laid dry. The walls are generally quite thick for added strength and insulation. Wood is used primarily for the interior structure, floors, and roofs. Joists and beams that can span reasonable distances support the flooring in multilevel buildings. Wood roof frames are reasonably light and easily assembled and may be covered in such materials as tile, stone, wood shingles, or thatch, depending upon local considerations. Simple pitched A-frame roofs, common in most Andalusian villages and in Swiss mountain houses, provide attic storage space that also insulates the living quarters. The combination of wood and masonry thus offers good, unobstructed interior space, strong and durable perimeter walls, and excellent insulation.

Masonry structures. All-masonry structures are found in places where little or no wood is available. The primary difficulty presented by this building type is the roof construction. Only a very limited distance can be spanned by a heavy stone lintel—which is also difficult to cut, move, and erect—and so builders had to invent alternative roofing methods. A variety of vaulting systems were developed to solve this problem, which are boldly expressed in the exterior form and can create interesting, high-ceilinged interior spaces. The basic vaulting systems include the barrel vault, groin vault, cupola, cone, and many of their variations. The additional bracing required to counter the diagonal stresses and outward forces of the roof leads to a considerable increase in the thickness of the supporting walls and to the development of an interdependent buttressing system among the habitations. This in turn influences the form of the village, since common supporting walls are the most economical and logical means of building where masonry roofs are necessary. Wood, where available in limited quantities, is used for roof scaffolding, and is reused throughout the construction of the village. Any additional wood is used for doors and framing.

MEDITERRANEAN TYPES

The Mediterranean basin generally lacks forests but is abundant in rock, stone, clay, and sand, and it has thus developed a vernacular architecture primarily of masonry. The climate is generally dry and temperate, and three dwelling types are common: patio houses with contained courtyards, terraced houses stepped down hillsides, and simple row houses that define street corridors on relatively flat land. The open courtyard style is found, with substantial variation, from North Africa to southern Spain to the Greek islands; it provides weather protection, privacy for work and recreation, and a flexible outdoor space for celebration, meditation, or work. The terraced house takes advantage of natural site conditions for light, view, and ventilation. The row house has a front or rear yard, projecting balconies, or a roof terrace for its outdoor space. Sometimes combinations of these unit types occur within one village because of terrain conditions, creating a complexity within the community, although one type usually predominates.

Mediterranean village plans vary with site conditions and historical development, but are linked by a formal unity and solidarity, an organic, additive nature of development, and a strong definition of the relatively dense urban structure and cubistic volumes. Modern conditions have altered the nature of traditional villages in some areas, as tourism, rather than agriculture or fishing, has become the dominant economic livelihood; many town characteristics are undergoing subtle changes. The market square or harbor has become more recreational, with additional cafés and restaurants. New shops have appeared along streets and passageways. The plasticity of stucco and whitewash over rubble has given way to the crisp definition of cement walls. Crooked, textured paving has been replaced by slick, machined surfaces. Although the influence of modern society is changing some areas, the village framework—both communal and architectural—remains strong, and the traditional village forms are surviving. This presents an important lesson for architects and planners today. Successful environmental architecture must permit, within its structure, minor compromises that express the will of individuals; simultaneously, its spatial organization and physical form must provide an overall unity, continuity, and permanence for community development. The Mediterranean village is an excellent, though regionally limited, example of diversity, of the association of unit form with individual needs, and of the spatial dynamics accorded human activity in relatively high-density living conditions.

MODERN ARCHITECTURE

Early modern architects reevaluated forced spatial disciplines, discarded superfluous applied decoration, and glorified new materials and manufacturing processes. Most chose to break completely with the past, ignoring their environment and thinking in completely fresh and new terms. But in so doing, they forgot the social and architectural lessons of traditional building. Thus, the revolution in architecture began. Innovators fought with the architectural establishment on one hand and the unaware and confused public on the other. Established bonds were broken; half a century later we still have not recovered.

LE CORBUSIER

Charles-Édouard Jeanneret—Le Corbusier—was one of the early leaders of the architectural revolution and is now universally known as one of its greatest architects. A particular interest in the Mediterranean basin led him to travel, search, discover, sketch, and interpret; he journeyed to Athens and the Acropolis, and to the Aegean Islands, where he discovered a public architecture that varied from island to island and that had been influenced by local conditions, trading, and past conquests. The bright sun, sharp shadows, and dynamic chiaroscuro of the area exposed a certain clarity of form and honesty of spirit, an architecture at once humble and magnificent. Even ideas from the Mediterranean region of Africa were suggested here in Greece; some of Le Corbusier's

1

works bear a striking physical resemblance to certain structures in North Africa, although he had not travelled there in his early career. He drew upon these experiences throughout his oeuvre, however, and not one of his buildings does not reflect in some manner, in some detail, his deep respect and understanding of the principles, as well as the physical forms, of Mediterranean architecture. As he wrote in *Towards a New Architecture*, "I have felt myself become more a man of . . . the Mediterranean, queen of forms under the play of light; I am dominated by the imperatives of harmony, beauty, plasticity."

2

In his 1948 designs for a vacation colony at Sainte-Baume along the Riviera in southern France (fig. 1), the repetitive, barrel-vaulted roofs relate directly to the simple, living-and-storage *ghorfa* structures of southern Tunisia (pages 158–159); his more refined design at Cap-Martin a year later resembles the more sophisticated vernacular dwellings on the Greek island of Santorini. In both examples, the roof forms create an overall harmony and rhythm, as well as a strong village identification, while the buildings' sweep into the hillside recalls many Mediterranean communities, such as the village near Tizi-n-Tichka pass in southern Morocco. In Le Corbusier's most creative design, the chapel at Ronchamp (fig. 2), certain forms have been borrowed from the vernacular architecture of Santorini, such as the bold projecting rainwater spouts and semicircular shafts; the free, sweeping plasticity at Ronchamp is closely related to the mosques on the island of Djerba, off Tunisia, and to the Paraportiani church on Mykonos (pages 68–69), all sculptural forms shaped and reshaped by humans and nature. Le Corbusier focused on the modest but comfortable interior spaces of the vernacular dwellings. For instance, the configuration of typical interiors on the Greek island of Skyros—a sleeping balcony extending over a kitchen-storage area within a large cubic house volume—was reinterpreted in an apartment house at Marseille to create a dynamic living area within the limits of the apartment bay.

Thus Le Corbusier absorbed the elements of Mediterranean community architecture into his designs, and was the first modernist to go beyond simple formal purification to a bold energy, sure hand, and fresh approach partially derived from and surely inspired by his Mediterranean experiences. The major elements that Le Corbusier integrated into his own work were the organic yet independent relationship of the village to the earth; the bold yet controlled expression of both plastic and simple geometric forms; the play of light upon surface; the subtle use of bright color; and the always evident human scale of building.

SEARCH AND RESEARCH

Le Corbusier was the first International Style architect to interpret and translate the spirit and forms of Mediterranean architecture; his important role in the development of modern architecture has in turn served as the vehicle for transmitting them to a wider audience.

In addition, other modernists traveled throughout the Mediterranean region, particularly to the Greek islands, and studied and analyzed the villages firsthand. These individual experiences should continue to lead to more personal interpretations of the traditional forms in the future.

The Mediterranean builders' intuitive, direct, and honest approach to creating a satisfying environment within limitations of climate, terrain, available materials, and structural knowledge is similar to the architects' search for imaginative designs that take economic and aesthetic advantage of modern techniques and materials to devise meaningful human environments. The examples of modern architecture presented here are thus intended to demonstrate the range of influences which have inspired and molded physical forms.

MODERN ARCHITECTURE
IN THE MEDITERRANEAN

In 1958, a violent earthquake on Santorini destroyed a large amount of housing; in 1960, a team of architects led by Constantinos Doxiadis designed new neighborhoods (fig. 3) sympathetic to the established island traditions (page 44) and located next to existing villages. Barrel-vaulted roofs express the major interior spaces; humanly scaled walls, paths, and terraces harmonize

with each other and with the older and more sculptural villages; boldly painted doors and windows puncture the thick walls. In addition, the older neighborhoods were rebuilt by their inhabitants in the traditional free, intuitive manner—a slow but certain process. Thus, the pattern of the original village has been preserved, the sympathetically designed new buildings form a new urban cluster, and the two related yet independent communities reinforce one another with a common scale, order, and sense of unity.

Near Badajoz, in southwestern Spain, José Luis Fernandez del Amo designed the new village of Vegaviana (fig. 4) to replace antiquated housing for local farm workers. The red-tiled roofs, pitched and rippled, and the whitewashed, stuccoed masonry walls are consistent with typical Andalusian architecture, such as that of Mijas (pages 96–97). In general, local environmental conditions—prevailing winds, rainy seasons, solar orientation—have influenced the unit design and the size and location of doors and windows. While the simple interior plans are closely related to the original structures, the village is unfortunately laid out in monotonous parallel rows. But it is likely that individuals, responding to their changing needs and new autonomy, will develop a more interesting physical expression.

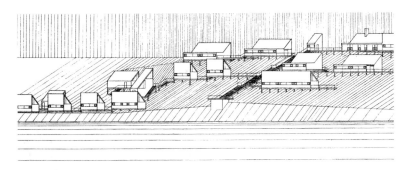

8

9

In Accra, Ghana, a group of young architects from the Division of Public Construction has designed the Junior Staff Quarters at Government House (fig. 5) in a style reminiscent of North African vernacular architecture. Modern materials and construction methods, such as concrete block for walls and poured reinforced concrete for floor slabs, have been used in an interlocking building form that is related to local tradition yet is uncompromisingly modern. The sharp articulation of the forms, deep visual penetration of the walls, and narrow, shaded areas are typical of many North African villages, such as Tinerhir (pages 144–145), a fortified town in the stone desert of Morocco. Although standard units are repeated, their clustered arrangement, varying in height, creates a rich formal interplay and experiential complexity. Thus, over a long period, an orderly plan of identical dwellings has achieved a result similar to an organic development.

MEDITERRANEAN INFLUENCES
IN MODERN ARCHITECTURE

The Mediterranean vernacular has proved fruitful in architecture beyond the Mediterranean region and its traditional building types, notably in housing, and particularly in northwestern Europe and in the United States. In 1961, near Bern, Switzerland, Atelier 5, a group of young architects who were former employees and associates of Le Corbusier, designed the Hallen Housing Estate (fig. 6). It is a series of tightly knit, cubistic masonry units sited in horizontal rows parallel to the contours of a hillside and connected by narrow alleyways and paths. The dwellings, with terraces and roof gardens, are reasonably private and individualized within, yet are attached, interrelated, and create a visual harmony. The natural siting, which takes advantage of the local terrain, is similar to designs employed by the popular builders of the farming community of Mijas (pages 98–99) in southern Spain. Another striking formal similarity exists between Hallen Housing Estate's roof gardens (fig. 7) and the roof terraces of Tinerhir, Morocco (page 147).

10

In 1958, architect Edward Larrabee Barnes designed the Haystack Mountain School of Crafts (fig. 8) on Deer Isle, along the rugged Maine coast. The box-like wood structures, sheathed in cedar shingles, are similar to the simple fishing shacks typical of the New England coast. However, the proximity of the units, disciplined plan, and organized spatial relationships constitute a controlled environmental statement and are more closely related visually to a grouping of dwellings and storage structures like that of Palheiros de Tocha (fig. 9), a Portuguese fishing village. Although the Haystack Mountain School is on a rocky and precipitous slope, and Palheiros de Tocha is on a flat, sandy shore, in each case the isolated, repeated forms clearly express the wood structure, relate well to the environment, and establish a formal unity.

11

In 1961, architect Paul Rudolph designed a housing village for married students (fig. 10) at Yale University in New Haven, Connecticut. The development, which had to be substantially simplified due to cost considerations and which, as a result, does not have the visual richness and unit privacy of the first scheme, was designed for a difficult, sloping site. Rudolph created an exciting, humanly scaled, three-dimensional form in brick and concrete, offering such amenities as private, walled gardens, stepped paths, and public courtyards. The interlocking massing of the cubistic volumes creates a dynamic complexity of related forms similar to

those of the intricate design of Tinerhir (pages 142–143). The spatial sequence and relationship to the local terrain are also similar to many Greek island towns. The informal repetition of the unit form lessens the project's impact, ties the buildings firmly to their surroundings, and enables the creation of varied spatial experiences and meaningful public areas.

In 1960, architect Yan Chun Wong designed two handsome clusters of one-story patio houses (fig. 11) for a Chicago neighborhood of three-story apartment buildings. Patio houses have, throughout history, provided protection, privacy, interior illumination, and ventilation for individual family units. But because of high land costs in urban areas, this type of low-density housing—usually of only two or three stories—is rarely constructed, even though, in specific circumstances, it is a viable alternative. In the Chicago project, each dwelling unit is separated from the street by a severe brick wall and

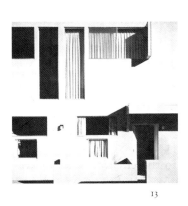

is brightly lighted by a private interior courtyard, which serves as a visual focus for all of the rooms and as an outdoor living center during the summer. Within the limits of the site, the design is successful; however, a larger development would have demanded considerable variety to offset the monotony of the continuous perimeter walls. A similar building system was fully realized in a Moroccan village near Khenifra (pages 148–149). Linear streets are defined between dwellings, and square private courtyards serve for work and recreation. In addition, the inhabitants use their flat roof surfaces for drying food and laundry.

Finally, in his designs for the dormitories of the Indian Institute of Management at Ahmedabad (fig. 12), architect Louis Kahn has worked in a bold scale and with simple but powerful repeated forms to establish a community structure of unusual dig-

nity and strength. In Ait-Benhaddou (pages 130–131) in the Moroccan desert, the imposing building cubes take command of the desolate landscape in a similar way.

DETAILING

In addition to the relationships between modernism and Mediterranean vernacular in village development and form, the expression of details in Mediterranean areas has served as the basis for a richness of fenestration and a humanization of scale without the introduction of applied decoration or sculpture. The details of good modern architecture, as do those of the vernacular, can both express function and serve as decoration. Moreover, they are the areas where individuals can leave their imprints on an anonymous design.

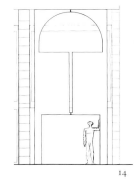

At the Monte Vista apartment project (fig. 13) in Monterey, California, for instance, by Moore, Lyndon, Turnbull, and Whitaker, the architects created a complex wall of fenestration in which door, windows, entrance canopy, and sunshields work together in a composite design. Similarly, the facade of a typical cave dwelling at Cuevas del Almanzora (page 120) in southern Spain is subdivided into a composition of interesting and related forms by the expression of internal functional needs.

In his 1959 design for a United States Consulate in Luanda, Angola (fig. 14), Louis Kahn used a protective, arched, T-shaped opening for ventilation and privacy and for admitting light while simultaneously reducing glare. A similar device is used in the underground dwellings of Matmata, Tunisia (page 154); the central section may be closed, and the arms used for decorative objects. In his scheme for a meeting house at the Salk Institute for Biological Studies (fig. 15) in La Jolla, California, Kahn designed a dynamic, double-walled facade of arches and rectangular openings as a sunscreen for the interior and also for a strong sense of wall envelopment. Kahn's facade, though designed in a limited time period, is quite similar to the rich facade surrounding the harbor at Procida, Italy (page 82), which was developed through centuries.

Landscape architect Paul Friedberg's 1964 designs for the Riis playground complex in New York City (fig. 16) recall the Mediterranean staircase, which is not only functional but social and recreational. In the playground, stair and plaza are integrated into a multilevel experience, similar to that of the front steps of a dwelling near Alberobello, Italy (fig. 17). In both cases, imagination and creative effort have transformed a utilitarian element into a rich, multipurpose form.

THE POTENTIAL OF PREFABRICATION

The mass production of prefabricated elements, from small components to complete structures, has been developed parallel to and is thus partly responsible for the direction of modern architecture and building techniques. But because of problems en-

18

demic to the industry in the United States—lack of public response, unions' concerns regarding automation—prefabrication has yet to fulfill its potential. Prefabricated structures could be the mechanism for designing and building new housing consistent with the principles of Mediterranean community architecture. Systems of flexible architectural units could solve the needs of rising concentrations. Buckminster Fuller explored these ideas in the 1930s, and the lightweight space frames and concentrated building packages that he pioneered are finally being developed into practical architectural design components. But these sys-

tems are not ends in themselves. They must provide variety, privacy, and all the amenities that traditionally built large structures do not—and at lower cost. They must also relate to, and complement, local building traditions and natural conditions.

DESIGNING NEW NEIGHBORHOODS

For years, younger architects and architecture students have been exploring the methods and means of creating complete neighborhoods. Based on his McGill University thesis project, architect Moshe Safdie designed the prototype of a total development pack-

19   20

age: Habitat, in Montreal (figs. 18, 19). This was the first attempt to design a complete neighborhood, and, therefore, is somewhat primitive. Its form resembles the pyramidal coastal town of Positano, Italy (pages 90–91). In addition, the individual dwellings, stepped and with terraces, are similar to the cubistic houses on the Greek island of Skyros (fig. 20). Habitat embodies the spirit, order, and principles of Mediterranean vernacular architecture, but still respects the economic and technical climates of to-

21

day; this is its strength. The project is not imitative; it does not try to emulate the picturesqueness of the Mediterranean region. Habitat instead extracts a totality, scale, and vision from its Mediterranean counterparts, and strives to create a pleasant human environment.

As a prototype, Habitat is not perfect. It is massive and heavy and lacks flexibility and spatial variety. But as an idea,

Habitat is sound. It demonstrates a complete reorganization of our system of building, and it lays the groundwork for the future of housing in our society. Habitat evolves directly from the building principles of Mediterranean community architecture, with the only changes in material and methods. The project is in this sense an experimental laboratory for the future of the urban environment.

UNIT DESIGN SYSTEMS

Unit systems may be made more economical through the refinement of light-weight, easily assembled structures. One approach is the flexible partition-and-slab system. Individual units are

22   23

brought to the site in small component parts and either assembled on grade and hoisted into position or assembled in place.

24

This method allows for easy transportation to the site, convenient replacement of defective parts, and considerable flexibility of interior planning. However, this system is only slightly more advanced than present construction methods; it has been used only with limited imagination and primarily for industrial structures, classrooms, small office buildings, and vacation houses. To make this technique more practical, larger portions must be preassembled and utility cores must be introduced.

A more promising prefabricated building system is the package unit, which can be completely factory-assembled on site, as was Habitat, or delivered whole from the factory. High-quality

units that plug into structural grids or stacks will ultimately provide the breakthrough for present housing needs. But the building industry has been resistant to this type of system because profitable construction methods would have to be completely reconsidered. To realize the package unit technique, units must be made lighter and more flexible, and a large-scale market must be created so that the units can be built economically.

25

Paul Rudolph has devised a unit system for multistory housing (fig. 21) that uses completely prefabricated units similar to mobile homes. The units are suspended by cables from platforms supported by central service shafts. Several living decks, with communal balconies, are grouped together on different levels. The heights of the housing clusters vary, depending on site and environmental conditions and on the need to create special vistas or variety among units.

Robert Oxman, of the Planning and Design Division of the Land Administration of Puerto Rico, has developed a planning and structural system for fishing villages in Puerto Rico (figs. 22, 23). Precast columns and beams form a three-dimensional skeletal grid that encloses standardized housing units and communal open spaces. Variations may occur within the basic modular system to provide inhabitants with an appropriate design framework for their particular needs.

26

In a prototype for a vacation village (fig. 24), the author has developed a system of prefabricated, fifteen- by fifteen-foot wood boxes with generous balconies and connecting bridges on a modular grid. The system can expand vertically or horizontally and can adjust to different terrain conditions. Standard sliding glass sections, metal circular stairs, and prefabricated kitchens and bathrooms fit into the structural shell. One- to four-story units can be arranged around central courtyards, for instance, or in isolated clusters.

URBAN CONTINUITY

Another consideration for unit building systems is their ability to form complete neighborhoods within established environments. The units must relate to existing grid patterns, transportation infrastructure, and dominant local buildings or groups of buildings. The systems must simultaneously serve as a link to the past, meet the needs of the present, and suggest a future course of development.

In a project for Philadelphia (fig. 25), architect Louis Sauer designed a series of town houses with alternating public spaces and private courtyards; this rich configuration of humanly scaled forms relates very well to the eighteenth-century town houses in the area. Several of these traditional buildings have been preserved on the site and have actually set the standard for the design. And the similarity between the Philadelphia project and a small square on the Aegean island of Mykonos (page 34) is also remarkable.

A housing project by the author along the East River in New York City (fig. 26) takes advantage of its site with a waterfront promenade that will serve as a park and marina with cafés and playgrounds. For centuries, the inhabitants of Coricella, on the island of Procida, Italy (pages 72–73), have congregated at a wide, water's-edge promenade that is also used by fishers to dry their nets and unload their vessels; it is still important to recognize the value of underutilized recreation land.

In a proposal by the author for housing in Brooklyn (figs. 27, 28), new buildings retain the traditional six-story scale of the neighborhood, and new entrances relate to local courtyards. In addition, street facades are simple in design and material, as are those

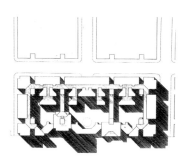

27

28

of nearby buildings. However, the interior of the double block opens onto a hierarchy of non-traditional outdoor spaces: porches, balconies, and roof decks, all within the design system, and a major central communal space.

VISIONS OF THE FUTURE

Beyond Habitat lie uncounted visionary proposals by architects around the world; many must wait until materials and construction methods are developed or refined. Japanese architects have been especially concerned with urban planning and housing because of the acute population density in and around Japanese cities. A team of architects led by Kenzo Tange has designed new neighborhoods for Tokyo that extend over Tokyo Bay (fig. 29). Trian-

29

gular structures containing neighborhood amenities and housing would be built on platforms over the water. Architect Noriaki Kurokawa has also been working to develop an evolutionary urban system that would accommodate growth and change. His Helix City proposal for Tokyo (fig. 30) consists of fan-shaped structures: totally self-sufficient neighborhoods connected by a monorail system. Another kind of urban megastructure has been designed by the author (figs. 31, 32). Flexible units develop as horizontal or vertical additive structures, and the major community spaces are expressed as singular forms that serve as identifying symbols and as a contrast to the modular design.

30

It is perhaps unfair to judge these visionary projects purely on their physical manifestations, since they are conceptual schemes rather than refined design statements. Nevertheless, their seemingly endless continuity can present a problem. Mediterranean towns have built-in limitations of site, size, and population; these limitations help the villages maintain their interest and diversity. Complete domination of an island or site by a continuous, unrelieved linkage of similar systems would destroy both the unique building systems and the overall village forms. The unending monostructures of many visionary designs can overwhelm the population they intend to liberate; the mass production of inferior copies, such as that of the Miesian glass box, is similarly dangerous. These disastrous results can be avoided by a careful examination of the limitations inherent in Mediterranean villages.

It is my hope that through a better understanding of the unit forms and village developments of traditional Mediterranean builders and through a deeper awareness and concern for the social needs of people today we may eventually solve the problems of modern housing and urbanism. It is clear that in the new building systems necessitated by population growth, we can evoke the spirit of the Mediterranean village not through imitation or romantic interpretation, but through the development of unit additive forms and our concern for the spiritual and spatial needs of people.

31

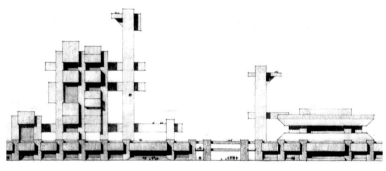

32

Repetition without monotony was characteristic of the earliest human settlements. The technical limitations of the past led to repetitive form in housing, and the advanced building techniques of the future will tend naturally to standardization. Whether these techniques will result in satisfying order or numbing monotony will depend on the sensitivity of architects to the needs for variety, privacy, and community identity. Whether their potential will be truly realized will depend on public awareness and support.

1969

GREECE

Architecture on the Aegean Islands of Greece attains a classical serenity, order, and dignity. Although the architectural unit forms vary from island to island, they are related through their subtle responses to and harmonious relationships with the natural surroundings, even though the brilliant white cubes are in sharp contrast to their dark rock bases.

The islands are varied in form and size; some are rugged and protective, others relatively flat and vulnerable. The communities were established for various purposes: defense, control, or open trade; each impetus structured the village forms differently. In general, there are two types: the defensive town high on a hill, such as Oia on Santorini, and the harbor village open to the sea, such as Mykonos.

The lack of forests and abundance of stone have produced a masonry architecture of considerable variety throughout the islands. Within this framework, individual artisans have expressed themselves with vivid color and imagination in the detailing.

Within the village structure, forms and plastic continuity are smoothly and easily associated. The exceptional building—most often the church or chapel—is not a focus but rather an integrated part of the whole village form or an isolated sculpture in the island plan.

Santorini

The subtle, motionless grace of the harbor town of Mykonos recalls the forms of nearby peninsulas and islands. A rich configuration of white cubes is concentrated around the active harbor and extends into the hills, terminating in isolated units. Urban density has been achieved for commerce and convenience rather than for defense. Unlike dense town forms limited by geographical or protective considerations, this former trading center opens to the sea traveler and gently extends into the rocky grazing pastures beyond.

The variety of spatial experience must come from within, since Mykonos does not have the dramatic site of so many other Greek island towns. But this situation is the ultimate advantage in the controlled movement and human scale of the endless streets. They sweep out from the harbor into alleyways and passages in a natural order, unified by the plastic continuity of whitewashed surfaces, with softened edges that ease the gaze from wall to wall. Streets are also enriched by exterior stairs, occasional bridges and tunnels, and small areas of intense color on wood doors, window frames, balconies, and railings. The many chapels of the village adhere to the order of the street; they express themselves, but do not dominate. Sometimes, a small neighborhood square forms an alcove that interrupts but never terminates the movement.

The typical dwelling is a two-story, masonry structure, with living spaces below and sleeping areas above. Each unit has an exterior staircase that contains storage or service space. Only infrequently do these modest row houses have rear yards or terraces; therefore, the small, simple interior spaces depend upon the narrow streets for light and air as the inhabitants depend upon the streets to extend their living quarters and as passages to the harbor or pasture land.

SERIFOS

The cubic dwellings of Serifos occupy a protective high point on the island and spill down gracefully toward the orchards below. In the past, the defensive village form was entirely concentrated on the difficult, craggy terrain around the cap of the hill, with views toward the distant approaches of enemies. Today, most of the upper village has been abandoned, and the more recent habitations step down the hillside to terraced farmland and the harbor. These dwellings are generally located along the leeward side of the hill, using it as a buffer against the strong winds. The terrain has, in effect, determined several neighborhood "finger" developments that stretch in opposite directions as the village continues to grow down the slope. Through this natural expansion the village has achieved a far more interesting form than it had in the past, and it has become an integral yet articulated part of its hill base instead of a dominating crown. The villagers have the advantages of good views, ventilation, and natural recreational facilities.

In modern times, volcanic eruptions and earthquakes have caused great physical change on the island of Santorini, known to the Greeks as Thira. It is full of dynamic contrasts, with rich soil of volcanic ash producing excellent wine grapes along the outer shore and sheer cliffs of formidable strategic importance dominating the interior bay. Although the outer edge of the island's crescent form slopes gently down to the sea, the inner edge drops abruptly some 600 to 1300 feet. Here, the towns of Phira and Oia have for centuries stood defiantly, protected from enemy attack, but in a constant war with nature for survival.

In response to the unstable nature of the island's topography and the ruggedness of its terrain, an architecture has developed of habitations linked by an interdependent buttressing system. Individual units are generally on different levels and are connected by sweeping walls and terraces, which serve to buttress the cliffs and anchor the dwellings. The repeated parallel diagonal lines of the jagged walls and the regularity of the vaulted roofs create unity and continuity in the free, organic plan. A town form has evolved that is at once plastic and sculptural.

The many levels are joined by complex stair configurations. Major streets—built for the stride of the donkey, the island's principal form of transportation—are stepped ramps zigzagging down the rugged slope to the small port below. Unlike the smooth, horizontal terracing of less steep hillside sites, these cliffs demand an angular interlocking architectural form.

The dominant design element in Santorini is the barrel vault. In the port the structures buttress one another in a row. In the upper villages they twist and turn freely, sometimes interlocking, sometimes terminating in a thick side wall. Openings are always at the ends of the dwellings, to maintain structural continuity, and generally are symmetrically composed of three windows around a central entrance door. Semi-cave dwellings and flat, terraced roof structures take advantage of the natural terrain.

Communal activity is encouraged by the linked terraces and their proximity to the vertical street systems. Families have reasonable privacy, yet participate easily in the interaction between the town and its port and share the distant vistas and dramatic views.

The town of Skyros in the Sporades is an example of a cubistic architecture that bends freely to the terrain, yet maintains a sophisticated order and unity. Since the village is on the hilly slopes of a great, rocky mound, the dwelling units sweep out in horizontal, concentric rings that conform to the land and define continuous curvilinear streets.

The community overlooks the island's rich olive groves and pasturelands. Its siting shelters it from the strong winds along the seaward side of the hill. In addition, the inhabitants have built on the least desirable agricultural land, but still take advantage of the excellent views and ventilation.

The dwelling cubes here, unlike those of Mykonos, are capped with roofs of a gray clay earth with good water-repellent and insulating properties. (Brilliant white roof surfaces would be unsuitable here because they would create a blinding glare in the town's upper neighborhoods.) Each unit's whitewashed exterior walls project above the roof to form a low parapet. Viewed from above, this cellular town structure distinguishes every building yet maintains the unity and continuity of the whole.

Many of the houses are one-room cubic chambers with high ceilings that provide space for interior wood sleeping balconies over storage and work areas at the rear. Most of the two-story dwellings are built into the hillside; direct access to the upper level is from a rear street or courtyard. The buildings, in straight rows, generally have rear yards, and semi-enclosed courtyards appear between clusters of houses. The occasional balcony is used for working and for drying clothing and food.

Most of the chapels are part of the street and are differentiated in roof form only by the addition of a small bell support above the street facade. Major churches are isolated from the dwellings by their own courtyards and serve as neighborhood visual focal points.

In the interior pasturelands of the island of Sifnos, eight small linked villages form an interconnected network of concentrated neighborhood nuclei separated by greenbelts of terraced farmland. Each town is built around a series of minor squares accentuated by churches or chapels, and the houses are informally arranged to conform to local topography. None of the villages occupies a strategic hilltop position because in the past fortified coastal towns defended the island. Therefore, an easy association of forms occurs within the groupings without the domination of any one village, and the hilltops are left bare except for an occasional windmill.

Compare this design to today's typical spread-out suburban developments around major towns and cities. The density is similar, yet on Sifnos the clustering of dwellings and villages creates a greater interaction of human experiences and affords generous open space between the neighborhood groups. Town and nature more than coexist; they support one another and interact to create a dynamic association of built and natural form.

In the ancient fortified village of Castro, a network of bridges, ramparts, and alleyways was constructed to defend the town against invaders who might have penetrated the perimeter walls. These have been modified in recent times to provide two-level access to dwellings. From the upper street, bridges connect to second-story entrance doors, creating an interesting visual experience and permitting generous natural lighting along the continuous alleyways below.

Throughout the Greek islands, and in sharp contrast to the continuity of the village units, churches or chapels serve as singular focal points within communities or as special pilgrimage places for an entire island. Usually these chapels were constructed in the sixteenth or seventeenth centuries by individual families for private worship, and they are relatively small. Nevertheless, their plastic and articulated forms and painted roofs distinguish them as pivotal or terminal points in the village or as dynamic isolated sculptures in the total island plan.

In Mykonos the churches are generally woven into the fabric of the community, and they heighten the experience of the street without terminating it. Similarly, on Santorini and Skyros they serve as occasional dominant elements within the whole of the village. The most varied and interesting groups of chapels, however, are found within the linked communities of Sifnos or at dynamic isolated points on the island. The often-repeated plan consists of one or two barrel-vaulted bays defining the major central space, with minor prayer apses and vestry and storage areas opening off and expressed from it. Sometimes twin chapels are harmoniously joined.

The thick stone-and-rubble walls are overlaid with stucco and whitewash. They are pierced by occasional clear glazed windows of moderate size, discreetly admitting light to the interior. The entrance doors, whether projecting or recessed, are well defined and elevated by several steps from the courtyard or street. Belfries are raised as the dominant elements in the facade.

Whitewash unifies the articulated elements in the overall structures into forms of great continuity; it is carried into the interior to reflect light. The painted wooden altars, lecterns, and pews become strong sculptural forms against the bare and undecorated interior surfaces, and the interiors are further brightened by the traditional, richly painted wooden iconostases typical of the Cyclades. Slate floor paving serves to unify the transition from exterior to interior and, in itself, is an important visual element. In the chapels at Sifnos, the paving joints are painted several times each year and are now considerably higher than the slate, strongly articulating the individual pavers. Occasional colored stones, in patterns that define burial positions, create rich and beautiful designs.

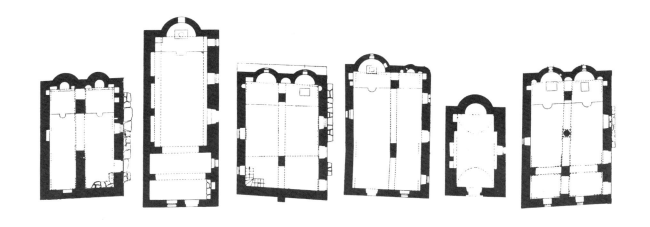

PARAPORTIANI CHURCH ON MYKONOS

The most unusual and inspiring church of the Greek islands is the Paraportiani Church. Actually a cluster of five chapels on two levels, it has been molded by nature and by humans to create a great plastic form of eternal poetry. The ground level consists of a row of three interconnected chapels, which are expressed strongly on the exterior, and a fourth interior chapel. The fifth chapel, on the second level, is reached by an exterior staircase and is covered by a perfect dome that gracefully terminates the complex. The belfry is the extension of a freestanding buttress that was once a wall. Together with additional supporting walls and buttresses, it completes the formal components. Humans, nature, and time have united to create a moving architectural monument.

ITALY

Italian Mediterranean architecture is abundant in variety and vitality. For this study, two diverse areas are of the greatest interest: the western coastal region in and around the Bay of Naples and the valleys of Apulia in the east, near Bari.

    The coastal villages near Naples were established by fishers; their dwellings either step down steep hillsides in horizontal layers or define harbors with walls of four- to five-story structures. These systems have enabled the fishers to observe the sea. Their families, in turn, can watch for their safety. The harbor is the focal point of the village and features a broad quay for communal work and social activities. Masonry is the major building material, presumably due to its durability, since wood is also available. Conceived with imagination and sensitivity, arch forms pierce the wall surfaces to create a variety of balconies, porches, and loggias, and stairways project in bold configurations. Each basic living unit is further defined on the exterior wall surfaces by soft pastel colors.

    In the valleys of Apulia, however, an agricultural society has cleared the land of stone to plant olive and almond groves and has created the unique, all-stone structures called *trulli,* with a conical form that goes back to neolithic civilizations. These unit structures usually occur as isolated clusters in the landscape; at Alberobello they form a complete village of sweeping visual continuity and dynamic human experience.

Procida

PROCIDA

Two fishing villages on the small volcanic island of Procida in the Bay of Naples offer double faces across the island's spine in response to quite different terrain. Although the buildings are of similar fenestration and color, the visual results are not at all alike. On one side, the port of Coricella steps down a steep hillside in a rich configuration of pastel-colored cubes that terminates in sweeping, projecting staircases on a wide, flat base. This base, protected from the sea by a stone jetty, serves as both a work surface for fishers and a promenade and social center for the whole village. Architecturally, it is a firm stop for the cascading dwellings, a transitional element linking the hill to the sea in the most useful manner, and a dramatic setting for the inhabitants. Roof terraces, recessed porches, and pathways interlock to form a dynamic interplay of solids and voids and to establish many levels of communal experience, offering private, semiprivate, and public spaces. Although individual buildings are expressed in different colors, and a variety of staircases responds to diverse needs, the strength and solidarity of the overall massing can support these distinctions, and the result is a monolithic village form.

On the opposite side of the island, the main port of Procida consists of four- and five-story row houses. Extending along the length of the harbor is a perforated outer wall, quite rich in form and variation, that has been molded to the changing needs of the inhabitants and that will continue to grow within a natural order. The visual expression of this order is experienced on three different levels: first, in the overall expression of community; second, in the relationship and grouping of forms within the homogeneous facade; third, in the penetration into the forms to uncover the elements of the ritual of daily life. The overall harmony has survived the conversion and adaptation of the original crescent and square forms into a complex system of diverse openings. Variation has replaced repetition; particular needs have induced changes that have transformed a simple geometry into a pattern of complexity and a tension of distorted forms. Semi-monumental apertures sometimes appear; scale is sometimes exaggerated. Within the total structure, free expression of the individual does not destroy the unity of the whole.

One of the earlier forms of human habitation is the cone. Various tent and thatch structures, self-braced, economically built, and generally portable, were developed by primitive peoples and are still used today. However, another type of less familiar conical construction exists: thick stone walls capped with a roof of concentric stone layers. Similar structures of prehistoric origin were developed throughout the Mediterranean basin, including the *lalajots* of the Balearic Islands and the *nuraghi* of Sardinia. The most complex and sophisticated—and still inhabited today—are the *trulli* dwellings of Apulia in southern Italy. Thousands of isolated farmhouses, generally formed of three to twenty units, dot the fertile almond and olive groves throughout the region.

The most complex development of this type of construction is found in the old Rione Monte section of Alberobello, where a series of narrow winding streets defined by *trulli* radiate from a central square. The unit structures buttress one another to form houses or groups of houses that open directly onto linear streets. Each *trullo* consists of a square or rectangular base topped by a conical, dry-stone roof with a chalk-coated finial. Although the sizes of the cones vary, the proportions are maintained, creating modulations in the repeated form. Square chimneys occasionally puncture the roof surfaces, offering additional contrasts to the uniform plasticity. Openings are limited to arched entranceways and small, square windows. Stuccoed and whitewashed, the stone walls can be as thick as five feet, providing good insulation and creating deep visual penetrations at the openings.

The domed interiors are plastered smooth and also whitewashed for good light reflection. The living space generally opens directly off the street and is surrounded by alcoves for cooking and sleeping. Sometimes wooden rafters support a storage attic or balcony over the major space. A fresh-water cistern below the house is fed by a roof drain and is reached from the interior by a bucket-and-pulley system.

In the large *trulli* houses, there is an interesting progression of movement from unit to unit, with subtle changes in the height of the domed ceilings, the size of the openings, and the form of carved niches in the wall surfaces. Small courtyards between dwellings serve as work spaces, and occasional projecting stairs, integral with the wall structure, lead to drying areas on the sloping roof surfaces.

POSITANO

The pyramidal town of Positano on the west coast of Italy, near Naples, consists of horizontal rows of pastel-colored dwellings stepping up a steeply angled hill that overlooks the beach and sea. Although it is today a well-known resort town, the overall form has been preserved, and the buildings, many of them altered from fishers' houses into private residences, shops, and hotels, have retained exteriors generally sympathetic to the original facades. Although the economic subsistence of the village has completely changed, it continues to maintain the dignity and strength of its original design. This is primarily due to the rigid respect for the natural horizontal terracing and the tight concentration of structures, which give an order and solidity to the village which balance the simple strength of the neighboring barren hills and promontories. The local church, at the shoreline, relates very well to the village because it does not disturb the continuity of the ringed concentration of dwellings but serves as a focal point in perfect harmony with it.

CORSICA

The town of Bonifacio, on the island of Corsica, is located atop a sheer cliff. The boldness of the buildings crowded up to the cliff edge matches the boldness of the site. Its limitations have led to a relatively high density of four- and five-story dwellings, no different from today's economically spurred, concentrated, vertical urban growth. The imposing shoreline composition has been achieved accidentally with the irregular fallen rock forms at the base, the sharp horizontal strata of the cliffs, and the vertical building cluster at the top. In this instance, severe contrast has evoked a dynamic visual response, yet the three elements work in unity to achieve a balance of total form. Such a chance determination of structure and organization is rare. While happy accidents occur frequently in our urban complexity, few attain such satisfactory results.

Bonifacio

SPAIN

The communities of Andalusia in southern Spain are united by common climatic and geological conditions which lead to similarities in construction materials and techniques. Stone supporting walls, stuccoed and whitewashed, and red-tiled pitched roofs over wood framing reappear regularly throughout the region. However, because of differing site conditions, a variety of village forms has been developed: free, adaptive plans on difficult sites; responsive terracing on hillsides; tight forms to free valuable farming land in valleys. In addition, the size and shape of the dwelling units vary in response to specific requirements. These factors have contributed to very different designs within a common denominator of material and structure.

Two contrasting examples are presented here. Arcos de la Frontera has developed freely around a hilly site, and its typical dwellings consist of rooms around private interior courtyards of great individuality and imagination. The farming community of Mijas, on the other hand, is built on a hill slope and has developed a linear form of parallel horizontal terracing.

In addition to the typical Andalusian village, there are two underground communities of special interest. The cave village of Guadix, near Granada, takes advantage of the earth as insulator and protector and sculpts its unusual natural environment to create an overall form of great plasticity, accentuated by clustered chimney forms. The underground community at Cuevos del Almanzora is composed of horizontal tiers of cave dwellings carved into the rock formations.

Mijas

94

MIJAS

The Andalusian farming village of Mijas consists of parallel rows of houses running along the contours of a steep hillside, facing a distant view of the Mediterranean. Because their depth is limited by the terrain, the houses present their broadsides to the elongated, terraced streets. The continuity of the whitewashed walls and the slightly offset red-tiled roofs further accentuates the horizontality of the village.

In the typical plan, the living room—as wide as the house and with a fireplace at one end—opens directly off the street. The kitchen, a sleeping alcove, and storage space are at the rear facing a yard cut into the hillside. Some of the houses are only one story high, but most have a second-floor attic, reached by an interior stair, that can contain additional sleeping rooms. Although party walls join similar houses, the walls have been built at different heights according to personal needs; this accounts for the clear differentiation and expression of individual units within the linear village form.

The traditional symmetrical facade composition—two windows flanking the entrance door, with a ventilation window above (also typical of Santorini in the Aegean Islands)—is altered for individual needs, giving additional diversity to the facades. Similarly, doors—usually of double width to permit better ventilation, interior lighting, and ease in moving large objects—are brightly painted and sometimes contain windows in one section. Openings are cut sharply into the thick walls to produce deep visual penetration. The roof overhangs keep rainwater away from wall surfaces and create additional sharp contrasts between roof and wall. Entrance steps vary from house to house, and many facades are decorated with hanging, painted tin cans holding plants.

Because of the linear village form, each house overlooks its neighbors, receives excellent light and ventilation, and enjoys both intimate and expansive vistas. The terraced rows of dwellings are connected by a steep, main street that leads to a major square.

BENALMÉDENA

This typical Andalusian village is nestled in a quiet valley in southern Spain, separated from its nearest neighbor by a wide greenbelt of orchards and farmland. The buildings are tightly concentrated so that a maximum of the valuable land can be used. The red-tiled roofs and whitewashed stucco walls create an order and unity while the free-form design bends to the natural terrain. Even the church responds to this order, although it is distinguished by its mass. The crooked streets work from the perimeter of the village into the central square, the focus of community life. Located tangentially to the highway, the village can expand at any point. This shows how clustered housing can free peripheral land for recreation and visual relief by using established land density for isolated structures.

This Andalusian hill town twists according to the natural terrain of a protective hill cluster at a bend in the Guadalete River. The dwellings themselves lack an obviously cohesive pattern yet are united by the similarity of the red-tiled pitched roofs and the whitewashed wall surfaces. They build up in mass to the churches that dominate the high points of the village. The crooked streets frequently change direction and join to form complex geometric intersections but generally lack the interest and strong character that they achieve in many of the villages in southern Spain. Entranceways, simple, uninviting, anonymous, and rectangular, and windows, lacking the vitality of traditional Andalusian ornamental ironwork, dominate the streets. However, within these austere facades unfolds a series of private interior courtyards, rich in variation and adapted to individual family needs. The two-story houses, separated by party walls, are built around these courtyards, with living spaces on the ground level, sleeping quarters on the second level, and a roof terrace above. The courtyard is the central focus and activity center, and all the rooms relate directly to it.

The dwellings share a common character. The street entrance opens onto a small, intimate vestibule, which in turn opens directly onto the courtyard. The courtyard is not large, but its white surfaces reflect light and brighten the perimeter spaces. A roof terrace, reached by exterior stairs, serves as a drying area and usually offers a dramatic view of the surrounding countryside. There are many variations within the central courtyards. Carved niches and extended platforms serve as work surfaces or for display. In addition, plants, clothing, and utensils are frequently hung along the wall, adding rich color and sculpture to the brilliant white surfaces. The major sculptural element is the stairwell, with red tile or gray slate used in different patterns. Especially impressive is the use of color and form. Numerous containers, mostly brightly painted tin cans holding different plants, enrich and complement the strong architectural surfaces of the space and create a very warm environment. Within the patio house, individuals have been permitted free expression. The experience of moving from house to house is one of constant surprise and delight.

VEJER DE LA FRONTERA

Vejer de la Frontera in southern Spain is a typical former defensive town; it crowns a hill site that continues to serve local farmers. The village is unified by whitewashed wall surfaces and terra-cotta roofing tiles; a single vertical church spire breaks through the horizontal form of the dwelling units. The town is isolated, surrounded by vineyards and orchards, and connected only by a solitary road to the passing highway. Of special significance is the procession from this highway. From a distance the town is framed by a pine forest; then the observer sees varying glimpses of the village from different positions during the approach and thus experiences continual visual surprises.

Contrast this with the singular lack of identification, interest, and surprise in the approaches to most of our towns and cities. We are universally greeted with endless chains of gas stations, eateries, and used-car lots. There is no gateway, only a town-limits sign. No superficial information station or "welcome" billboard can substitute for a genuine and meaningful spatial sequence such as that of Vejer de la Frontera.

GUADIX

The foothills of the Sierra Nevada mountains in southern Spain are a region of extraordinary character. The weather has eroded tufa hillocks into curious shapes, many of them conical mounds. In this area, a tribe of Gypsies has scooped caves out of the hillside and established an underground community of some ten thousand people. The cave dwelling is the earliest and most natural of human habitations; the advantages of subterranean living are obvious. However, the unique characteristic of this particular village is the ingenious way in which the inhabitants have molded the earth to their needs and imposed an order of design while still respecting the environment. From a distance, the village is only vaguely identifiable by the exposed entrances and chimneys of the dwellings, accentuated with whitewash. The rugged terrain of soft limestone, clay, and loam seemingly remains unspoiled and natural yet has been shaped by the residents.

The streets have a flowing, sculptural quality, brought about by the relationship between the built forms and the natural rock formations, which creates a variety of spatial contrasts. Most of the dwelling units are simple, connected cells; however, some contain as many as twenty chambers, and others have been enlarged by building exposed additions with red-tiled roofs and white stucco walls. Chimneys shoot up singly or in clusters, forming the major repetitive visual order of the village.

Interiors generally consist of well-tamped earth floors and whitewashed wall surfaces. The chimneys ventilate the interior space, and, where possible, small windows have been cut into the natural vertical surfaces for additional light and ventilation. The typical cave habitation is generally more nature than architecture. The village of Guadix, on the other hand, expresses a balance between art and nature and presents humans as earth sculptors.

CUEVAS DEL ALMANZORA

Another type of Andalusian underground community exists at Cuevas del Almanzora. Here, parallel rows of cave dwellings have been carved out of rocky cliffs to form three-story apartment buildings around large public squares. The size of the squares varies according to the terrain. The uneven cliffs and irregular apertures of the housing units are softened and linked by bands of whitewash, which accentuate the horizontality of the terracing and clearly differentiate the levels.

MOROCCO

The roots of Mediterranean community architecture in Europe can be traced to the cubistic farmhouses and villages found in the vast stretches of south and central Morocco. However, in Morocco there are two major differences. First, the local building materials—sand, stone, and red earth—are left unaltered; thus, a close association of village form with natural environment is emphasized, and the towns sometimes blend almost completely into their surroundings. Second, height, so necessary for defense in the relatively flat terrain of southern Morocco, is expressed by a taller and larger architecture than that of comparable European villages. Nevertheless, the Moroccan village and, more particularly, the *kasbahs* and *ksours* of the south are formal paradigms transported by Moorish trade and conquest to a large part of the Mediterranean basin.

Within Morocco, climatic and geographic extremes determine the various structures and forms of the villages. In the temperate climate of the hill and mountain areas, an architecture has developed in which flat, overhanging roofs serve as shelters and work surfaces and interlock to unite the village plan. However, in the hot and very dry climate of the flat stone desert, the architecture has great solidity and sometimes attains a strength of form that dominates its natural environment. Protection from both enemies and the elements were primary forces behind the design of these desert villages; therefore, a complex organization of towers, walls, and interlocking structures serves as both defensive labyrinth and shelter from the harsh sun and desert wind. The protective wall structure dominates the architecture as it weaves, enfolds, and finally unites the elements into a powerful total form.

Central Morocco

VILLAGE NEAR TIZI-N-TICHKA PASS

In the High Atlas Mountains near the Tizi-n-Tichka Pass, which links Marrakech to the stone desert of Morocco, a terraced Berber village gently slopes down a hillside and overlooks the nearby valley where its inhabitants farm the land. The village is on the barren lower slope of a mountain, high enough for protection, yet close to the fields. Systems of terraced levels have been employed in both village and fields. The terraces not only offer convenient level surfaces for building or farming but also establish a consistent linear, horizontal town pattern that ties into the contours of the landscape.

The interlocking houses are generally of two stories, with living quarters on the second level and animal shelter and storage below, all within one cubic shell. Each family has its own front yard, reached by paths perpendicular to the hill slope; depending upon the terrain, there are some small, private interior service courts within or between buildings. The uncluttered, flat roof surfaces, which actually form additional stepped terraces, are used for drying food and other materials and are occasionally pierced by small chimney openings. On the ground floor, each house has a large square opening, big enough for animals and large carts, that serves as the only entrance. On the second level, one roughly squared window on each exposed surface wall provides light and ventilation for the living spaces. These windows are heavily framed and protected from the weather with stucco and whitewash and are the strong decorative elements in the facade.

Unlike most isolated areas of the Mediterranean, a variety of building materials was available here, and the inhabitants were free to choose appropriately for their building construction. Walls are of stone, stuccoed for weather protection on the upper levels and left in exposed slabs below. This horizontal division expresses visually the separate interior functions. In the interior, wood is used primarily for lintels, floor and roof supports, and upper flooring. Thick protective roofs of mud and thatch overhang the walls to permit good drainage during the frequent rainstorms. The nature of the roof construction creates soft, rounded surfaces of extreme plasticity that offer a sharp contrast to the articulated wall surfaces below. The roofs are also the unifying element in the total design, weaving the terraced dwelling units of the village plan into a form of great continuity and cohesion, which gracefully extends into the surrounding natural environment. Such a village system could be naturally extended in any direction.

VILLAGE IN THE OURIKA VALLEY

A fan-shaped cluster of dwellings nestled into the terrain distinguishes a small village along a hillside in the valley of the Ourika River in southern Morocco, near Marrakech. Although there is no special hierarchy of building and the unit of habitation is a simple, cubic volume, the overall form is one of great unity, richness, and solidarity. Within the village, a series of community spaces defined by the dwellings steps irregularly down the hillside, linked by narrow passages. The buildings themselves, with their sharply defined, flat, overhanging roofs, also step down the slope, but in horizontal layers that parallel the natural contours of the hill. The synthesis of this building order is an absolute formal expression that is firmly tied to the land. In addition, the walls of rubble and earth and the roofs of mud and thatch serve to meld the village and the natural environment into an organic, monolithic entity.

AIT-BENHADDOU

Between the High Atlas and the Anti Atlas mountains in southern Morocco, in the Dades River valley, towering silhouettes of *kasbahs* and *ksours* dominate the exotic landscape of the stone desert. Most of these fortified villages rise above the flatlands in the valley, forming a continuous procession of cubistic geometry. However, near the oasis of Ouarzazate, at the valley's eastern approach, stands an unusual village of towers and walls that steps up the slopes of a hill and overlooks the dry riverbed of the Asif Mellah. In times past this fortified village, called Ait-Benhaddou, both protected and exploited camel trade caravans as they moved from the desert regions to the city of Marrakech.

The town plan consists of a series of *kasbahs* interconnected by lower structures and protective wall enclosures. This arrangement offered protection from both tribal enemies and the torrential flooding that still occasionally occurs along the path of the riverbed. The crowding of the crenellated towers and their terraced organization up the steep slope combine to form a powerful, soaring vertical effect, similar to the spirit of today's skyscraper cities, yet with a comprehensive order and monumental dignity. The small doors and windows and the vertical, pointed decorative recesses further emphasize the superscale form, and although not taller than forty or fifty feet, the towers give the illusion of much greater height.

The basic *kasbah* plan—a large, square central space with four square corner towers—is fused with lower structures to create a rich and complex multilevel town plan. The uniform red-earth color and the repetition of cube and tower give an order and unity to the village. The structures are primarily of mud and straw bricks, with occasional palm-trunk supports in the interior. Because of the thick, insulating exterior walls and narrow openings, the interior spaces are dark and intimate. Since this town was conceived as a fortification, there are endless mazes within the village walls. Many streets terminate abruptly in dead ends. Small squares and yards and narrow, crooked streets provide outdoor protection from the intense heat and desert sand- and windstorms. This quality of space gives a necessary psychological security to the inhabitants of this harsh environment.

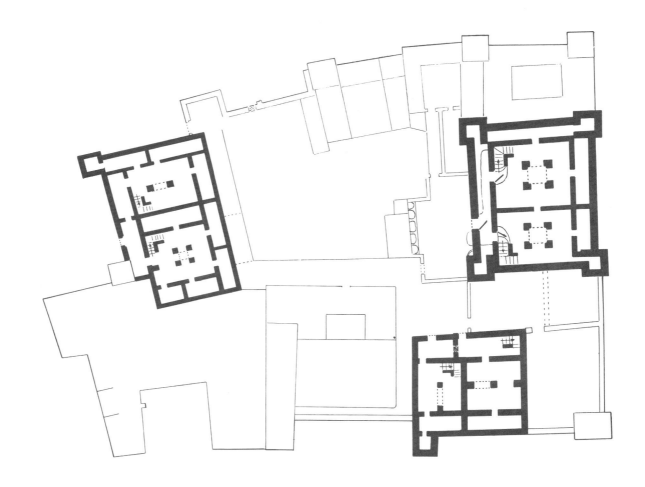

KSOURS IN THE DADES VALLEY

Along camel trails in the valley of the Dades are many varieties of *ksours,* or fortified villages. While the group of towns is related by material and function, individual communities have different characters. Some suggest lookout towers and the softened edges of pinnacled corners; others are composed of simple, crisp, interlocking cubes, severe and defiant. Some are expansive, enveloping large courtyards within a protective skin; others are as tight in plan and form as a modern urban apartment house. Therefore, although the village architecture of the river valley is consistent in material and purpose and creates a unified sequence of movement along the camel trails, the contrasting forms and sizes of the villages provide local identification and visual relief.

At the western end of the valley of the Dades, in the midst of an arid stone desert, lies the oasis of Tinerhir. Fertile green fields and a palm forest are embraced by a wall of dwellings, which separates the harsh, arid landscape from the rich productive soil within. The habitations are the red-earth color of the surrounding flatlands yet are distinguished by a sharp articulation of intersecting forms that creates a rich, crisp, geometric chiaroscuro.

The village plan is unique, as its major focus is the large negative central space. The perimeter ring of buildings accentuates the special nature of the oasis green, which also serves as the community's grand courtyard. Its symbolism as well as its practical role—harvest center—satisfies both physical and spiritual needs. Although the spatial form may be compared to a modern city's large public park or green, the contrast here is more intense and the psychological impact more satisfying, since the oasis supplies not only an area for recreation but the water and food essential for survival.

The houses are generally of two or three stories, with corner towers that project an additional story. The walls of adjoining structures intersect to brace one another and create not only an interlocking system of buttressing but also a pure form of great continuity and solidarity. Small openings, multiple rainwater spouts, and an absence of exterior decoration emphasize this quality.

Interiors are divided into intimate, dark spaces insulated from the harsh climate by the thick masonry walls of mud brick, rubble, and stucco. Roof terraces are used for the seclusion of women, as dictated by Islamic custom, and as drying areas and comfortable sleeping quarters. They also once served as an intricate network of escape during enemy attacks but now offer pleasant views of the central green and distant landscapes.

Deep pockets and narrow passages between the buildings can open onto public squares, providing visual relief and psychological security, as well as comfortable shade for the inhabitants. In addition, they form intriguing corridors which link endless stretches of the surrounding desert to the lush green oasis.

VILLAGE NEAR KHENIFRA

One-story atrium houses are the dwelling units in this small village, built along a stream near Khenifra in central Morocco. Building plots are regular square units, but the size of the enclosed courtyards varies; thus a diverse series of solids and voids is created. Privacy and protection are achieved in this simple, economical, gridded system. The major negative spaces, which in most villages are centrally located, are broken down into private cells within the individual habitations. Straight streets run between the unit groups to a wider avenue that parallels the adjacent stream. The communal spaces are linear and occur primarily along the riverbank. (The overall plan of this village is similar to that of Matmata, Tunisia, and its earth-cavity dwellings.) Flat roofs of mud and thatch are for drying food and clothing and are reached by ladders from the interior courtyards. Roof overhangs provide rain drainage away from wall surfaces, and the exposed structural timber beams supply a textured and decorative roof edge.

TUNISIA

No particularly uniform relationships exist among the villages of Tunisia. In response to climatic and geographic variations, a diverse collection of forms and communities has developed, some among the most original settlements of the Mediterranean region. In the temperate north, village forms are derived from the repetition of the atrium house; the most interesting is the Berber village of Takrouna, located atop a plateau cluster. The barrel-vaulted dwellings, with white, reflective roofs and natural walls, are located around courtyards and protected from the strong winds.

In the hot, dry south, a variety of solutions results from geographic differences. In desert areas, some villages consist of isolated rectangular houses that are sited parallel to prevailing winds, as at Kebili. Where stone is available, rough barrel-vaulted dwellings and storage chambers called *ghorfas,* as tall as six or seven stories, form protective, oval village clusters. Many villages are cut into the rock cliffs in the mesa region, and an entirely artificial cave community exists at Matmata, where the inhabitants have burrowed into the soft earth.

In addition to the mainland villages, the minor mosques of Djerba, a flat, palm-groved island off the coast, are of considerable interest. These isolated structures are diverse, plastic, sculptural forms. They serve as centers of pilgrimage throughout the island and as reference points in its plan, in the same way that the town square or exceptional building serves the village.

Gabes

MATMATA

In the arid lowlands of southern Tunisia is a unique village of caves built around large artificial cavities in the earth. They were originally excavated and inhabited by cave dwellers from the mountains and are among the more economical systems of permanent built housing.

The craters vary in size from twenty feet deep and forty feet across to thirty feet deep and two hundred feet across. The floor of each crater is connected to the surface with a long, gently sloping tunnel. At the midpoints of these passages are large, hollowed chambers for food storage or animal shelter. Caves dug into the vertical sides of the cavity serve as living quarters and additional storage rooms.

The area's dry sandstone is firm and extremely workable, easing this extensive burrowing into the earth as well as providing natural insulation and protection. Since the surrounding land was untouched, hostile tribes would pass at a distance, unaware of the village, and at times of siege, the entrances to individual tunnels could be readily secured.

Several thousand people live in Matmata today. Each crater houses up to one hundred inhabitants and serves as a natural front yard, rear yard, and storage and community space. The size of the public area varies in proportion to the population. While there is some danger of flooding and cave-ins from the infrequent rainstorms, daily life is uninterrupted during the violent windstorms endemic to the area.

The village plan includes a sophisticated communications network and a consequent abundance of spatial experiences. At ground level, the natural surface between the cavities, with an uninterrupted view of sky and horizon, acts as the street; the connecting tunnels are dark and intense; the public area is contained yet light and open; the perimeter living spaces are quite intimate. Throughout the day, inhabitants experience light and dark, intimacy and expansion.

GHORFAS AT METAMEUR AND GHOUMRASSEN HADADA

The tribes that once inhabited the mountain regions of southern Tunisia were forced to migrate to the valleys because of a lack of food and water and grazing land for their goats. They had lived only in mountain caves, and re-created this protective environment in the lowland areas with the available building materials and their limited building experience.

These tribes developed simple, barrel-vaulted stone structures called *ghorfas,* with small, dark, deep interiors that echoed the intimacy and security of their natural cave dwellings. The *ghorfas* were arranged in both vertical and horizontal rows to form walled enclosures defining large, oval courtyards that provided a protected gathering place during periods of siege and a marketplace during times of peaceful trading. Occasionally, these tribal neighborhoods were grouped to form a village, as at Medenine, where only isolated groupings now remain. More often, they took advantage of protective terrain by building around a hill, as at Metameur.

The *ghorfa* unit is both dwelling place and storage chamber, with living quarters on the first level and a storage attic above. At one time the *ghorfa* stacks reached a height of six or seven stories; generally, only two- or three-story segments exist today. The courtyard end of the unit features one central rectangular doorway per bay; upper levels are reached by an exterior staircase of projecting stones. The outer end of the unit is entirely closed; in modern times, however, some small openings have been pierced in order to ventilate the interior spaces. Each cell stands in complete isolation, with no interior connections disturbing the self-buttressing structural system. In some *ksours,* once the perimeter defense wall was erected, an increase in population or a good harvest dictated the building of additional units within the security of the plaza space, and thus a network of streets and alleyways has replaced the large public square, as at Ghoumrassen Hadada.

It is interesting to observe the variations in scale and spatial development that are possible within the framework of an unvarying unit architecture. The large public square at Metameur, in contrast to the tight individual cells of the *ghorfa,* offers a grand space for community experience. At Ghoumrassen Hadada, a height of two stories is appropriate for the narrow streets; anything higher would have considerably impaired sunlight and ventilation. In both places, the unit repetition creates an order and unity for individual buildings and for the village plan; meanwhile, imperfections in building methods and spatial definition prevent monotony.

TAKROUNA

About fifty miles south of Tunis, the Tunisian plains are interrupted by a cluster of three plateaus. Centuries ago, the Berbers built the village of Takrouna on these plateaus as a stronghold against Arab invaders. Villagers continue to live on and around this rare geological formation, where they overlook their fields and olive groves as well as the distant Mediterranean.

The village is composed of three neighborhoods on different levels, each with a separate view of the plains. A camel trail approaches from the plain, pauses at the first level of the village, and spirals past the second to reach the topmost level, built on a rugged, projecting plateau, thus creating a unique series of spatial experiences.

The village has been constructed almost entirely from the repetition of a single distinct architectural unit—a barrel-vaulted, one-story, rectangular block—which unites the three levels into a consistent whole. Stone is used for walls and vaulting, both because wood is scarce and because stone offers the maximum protection against heat and cold; a thick coat of white stucco reflects sunlight and reduces fierce winds. A short transverse vault at the center of each unit adds structural rigidity and emphasizes the central doorways.

In plan, Takrouna's dwelling blocks form closed courtyards, offering protection from the winds sweeping in from the plains and privacy for family groups. While basically square, the courtyards have been distorted in many cases to fit constricted sites. Twisting, narrow stone streets between these enclosures provide additional shelter from the wind. Street facades are severe, defined only by the entranceways and occasional small, high, ventilation openings. On the courtyard faces are larger windows and doors. The roofs provide ideal surfaces for drying food and laundry.

There is a unique spatial relationship among the three neighborhoods, with no special hierarchy. Each is roughly the same size, has a uniform organization and building unit, and occupies a separate plateau. Throughout the village are views up toward projecting cliffs, up or down to other parts of the village, or out across the plain. There is at once the intimacy of protective enclosure and the exhilaration of dynamic open space. From the plain, the village seems to have been boldly sculpted from the rock formation. From above, the interlocking buildings form a design system that relates to the order and organization of the orchards below and to the natural configuration of the distant mountains.

On the sandy, palm-groved, flat island of Djerba, off the southern Mediterranean coast of Tunisia, stand approximately three hundred mosques dedicated to two Muslim rites, Malekite and Wahabite. Some, such as the Mosque of the Turks at Houmt Souq, are monumental and are located within a village. However, a great variety of humble mosques, unrelated directly to a village but connected by lines of communication and pilgrimage, are strong focal points throughout the overall island plan. Just as a singular building within an urban community serves as a focus and pivot point, these structures are the physical and spiritual nuclei of this small island.

Among the structures is considerable variation in physical form, the demands of the rituals that dictate the spaces and their organization notwithstanding. A walled outer court with one entrance serves not as a protective barrier, as in traditional mosque design, but as a definer of space, establishing a welcoming atmosphere. This outer court is an important facility where outdoor prayer ceremonies are held and pilgrims eat and rest. The mosque is placed rather centrally within the outer court, and minor perimeter structures act as shaded porticoes for visitors and as storage facilities. A well and related canal system and prayer niches along the perimeter wall provide the minor court sculpture.

The mosque building itself is a large prayer room defined by square, regularly vaulted bays that are supported by a grid of columns. The entrance door is centered, and a smaller interior door leads to the minaret tower. Light enters only through the entrance door and very small slot windows. The structure is primarily of baked clay and stucco, as are most of the island's buildings. On the exterior, the vaulted roofs are either boldly revealed or concealed within the parapet of thick perimeter walls. Interior prayer niches are reflected in apse projections around the base, and pier buttresses of varying sizes brace and reinforce the shell. Another important part of the overall form is the exterior stairway, leading to an outdoor prayer platform attached to the building wall.

These expressive designs, stuccoed and whitewashed, form varied and beautiful structures of great plasticity. All are quite different, yet each is a strong and serene architectural statement.

In quiet places reason abounds;
that in quiet people there is a
vision and purpose, that
many things are revealed
to the humble that are
hidden from the great.
I hope and pray that I can
remember the great truths
that seem so obvious here
but so obscure in other places.

Adlai Stevenson

Illustration Credits

Numbers refer to page numbers.
Dan Forer, 10
Norman McGrath, 11 (top right, bottom left, bottom right)
D. Vassiliades, 64
D. Jacques-Meunie, from *Architectures et Habitats du Dades*
    (Paris, 1962), 132
Tunisian Department of Tourism, 156

Numbers refer to figure numbers in the introduction.
Le Corbusier, 1
Lucien Hervé, 2
José Luis Fernandez del Amo, 4
Government of Ghana, 5
Atelier 5, 6
Albert Winkler, 7
Edward Larrabee Barnes, 8
Paul Rudolph, 10, 21
Yan Chun Wong, 11
Satsango, courtesy National Design Institute, Ahmedabad,
    India, 12
Morley Baer, 13
Louis Kahn, 14, 15
David Hirsch, 16
Scott Ross, 18, 19
Robert Oxman, 22, 23
Louis Sauer, 25
Kenzo Tange, 29
Noriaki Kurokawa, 30